D0755840

sweet
puddings
& pies

THE AUSTRALIAN Women's Weekly

CONTENTS

AUSTRALIAN CUP AND
SPOON MEASUREMENTS
ARE METRIC.
A CONVERSION CHART
APPEARS ON PAGE 77.

It's exciting that puddings and pies are returning to our tables. Not only are they delicious and simple to create, many can be prepared ahead of time, which make them ideal for entertaining. Keep a supply of good quality vanilla ice-cream in the freezer and you'll have the perfect pairing every time.

Pamela Clark

Food Director

CLASSIC STEAMED CHRISTMAS PUDDING

prep + cook time 4 hours 30 minutes (+ cooling) serves 12

3 cups (450g) chopped mixed dried fruit
¾ cup (120g) finely chopped seeded
   dried dates
¾ cup (120g) finely chopped raisins
¾ cup (180ml) water
1 cup (220g) firmly packed light brown sugar
100g (3 ounces) butter, chopped
1 teaspoon bicarbonate of soda (baking soda)
2 eggs, beaten lightly
¾ cup (110g) plain (all-purpose) flour
¾ cup (110g) self-raising flour
1 teaspoon mixed spice
½ teaspoon ground cinnamon
2 tablespoons dark rum

1 Stir fruit, the water, sugar and butter in medium saucepan over heat, without boiling, until sugar dissolves; bring to the boil. Reduce heat; simmer, uncovered, 6 minutes. Stir in soda. Transfer mixture to large bowl; cool.
2 Stir eggs, sifted dry ingredients and rum into fruit mixture.
3 Grease 2-litre (8-cup) pudding steamer; spoon mixture into steamer. Top with pleated baking paper and foil (to allow pudding to expand as it cooks); secure with kitchen string or lid.
4 Place pudding in large boiler with enough boiling water to come halfway up side of steamer. Cover with tight-fitting lid; boil for 4 hours, replenishing water as necessary to maintain water level. Remove pudding from boiler; stand pudding 10 minutes before turning onto plate. Serve with cream, if desired.

tips To store, wrap room-temperature pudding in plastic wrap; refrigerate in cleaned steamer, or seal tightly in freezer bag or airtight container. Pudding can be stored in refrigerator up to two months or frozen up to 12 months. To reheat, thaw frozen pudding three days in refrigerator; remove from refrigerator 12 hours before reheating. Remove from plastic wrap and return to steamer. Steam for 2 hours following instructions in step 4.

PUDDINGS

CLASSIC BOILED CHRISTMAS PUDDING

prep + cook time **6 hours 30 minutes (+ cooling)** serves **12**

4 cups (750g) mixed dried fruit
1⅓ cups (185g) seeded dried dates, chopped coarsely
1¼ cups (185g) raisins, chopped coarsely
1½ cups (375ml) water
¾ cup (165g) caster (superfine) sugar
1 cup (200g) firmly packed light brown sugar
250g (8 ounces) butter, chopped
1½ teaspoons bicarbonate of soda (baking soda)
3 eggs, beaten lightly
¼ cup (60ml) dark rum
3 cups (210g) firmly packed fresh white breadcrumbs
1¾ cups (260g) plain (all-purpose) flour
2 teaspoons mixed spice
1 teaspoon ground cinnamon
60cm (24-inch) square of calico
⅓ cup (50g) plain (all-purpose) flour, extra
2.5m (2.5 yards) kitchen string

1 Stir fruit, the water, sugars and butter in large saucepan over heat, without boiling, until sugar dissolves; bring to the boil. Reduce heat; simmer, uncovered, 8 minutes. Stir in soda; cool.
2 Stir egg, rum, breadcrumbs and sifted dry ingredients into fruit mixture.
3 Fill a large boiler three-quarters full of hot water, cover; bring to the boil. Have string and extra flour ready. Wearing thick rubber gloves, drop pudding cloth in boiling water; squeeze excess water from cloth. Spread hot cloth on bench, rub extra flour onto cloth 40cm (16 inches) in diameter, leaving flour a little thicker in centre.
4 Place pudding mixture in centre of cloth. Tie cloth tightly with string as close to mixture as possible. Knot two pairs of corners together.
5 Lower pudding into boiling water. Cover with tight lid; boil 6 hours, replenishing water as necessary to maintain water level.
6 Lift pudding from water, place in large colander; cut string, carefully peel back cloth. Turn pudding onto a plate; carefully peel away cloth, cool. Stand 20 minutes before serving.

tips You'll need a 60cm (24-inch) square of unbleached calico for the pudding cloth. If the calico hasn't been used before, start with an 80cm (16-inch) square of calico, soak in cold water overnight. Next day, boil it for 20 minutes, rinse in cold water and cut to a 60cm (24-inch) square. To store pudding, we prefer to remove the cloth rather than hanging the pudding, as mould can form in our climate. After removing cloth, allow pudding to come to room temperature; wrap in plastic wrap and seal tightly in a freezer bag or airtight container, and refrigerate for up to two months.

college puddings

COLLEGE PUDDINGS

prep + cook time **40 minutes** makes **4**

⅓ cup (110g) raspberry jam
1 egg
½ cup (110g) caster (superfine) sugar
1 cup (150g) self-raising flour
½ cup (125ml) milk
25g (¾ ounce) butter, melted
1 tablespoon boiling water
1 teaspoon vanilla extract

1 Grease four 1-cup (250ml) metal moulds;
divide jam among moulds.
2 Beat egg and sugar in small bowl with
electric mixer until thick and creamy. Fold in
sifted flour and milk, in two batches; fold in
combined butter, water and extract.
3 Top jam with pudding mixture. Cover each
mould with pleated baking paper and foil
(to allow puddings to expand as they cook);
secure with kitchen string.
4 Place puddings in large saucepan with
enough boiling water to come halfway up sides
of moulds. Cover pan with tight-fitting lid; boil
25 minutes, replenishing water as necessary to
maintain level. Remove puddings from pan;
stand puddings 5 minutes before turning onto
plate. Serve with cream.

SOFT-CENTRED
MOCHA PUDDINGS

prep + cook time **40 minutes** makes **6**

155g (5 ounces) dark eating (semi-sweet)
    chocolate, chopped coarsely
125g (4 ounces) butter, chopped
3 teaspoons instant coffee granules
2 eggs
2 egg yolks
⅓ cup (75g) caster (superfine) sugar
¼ cup (35g) plain (all-purpose) flour
2 teaspoons cocoa powder

soft-centred mocha puddings

1 Preheat oven to 200°C/400°F. Grease
six-hole (¾-cup/180ml) texas muffin pan well
with softened butter.
2 Stir chocolate, butter and coffee in small
saucepan, over low heat, until smooth; cool
10 minutes. Transfer to large bowl.
3 Beat eggs, egg yolks and sugar in small
bowl with electric mixer until thick and creamy.
Fold egg mixture and sifted flour into
barely-warm chocolate mixture.
4 Divide mixture among pan holes; bake
12 minutes.
5 Gently turn puddings onto serving plates,
top-side down. Dust with sifted cocoa powder;
top with fresh raspberries, if you like, and
accompany with softly whipped cream.

tips These puddings should be served shortly after
they come out of the oven. Use a good-quality dark
chocolate with 70% cocoa solids.

pear charlottes with fig syrup

PEAR CHARLOTTES WITH FIG SYRUP

prep + cook time **1 hour** makes **4**

5 large pears (1.8kg)
1 cup (220g) firmly packed light brown sugar
1 cinnamon stick
1 cup (250ml) water
16 slices day-old white bread (720g)
90g (3 ounces) butter, melted
4 dried figs, sliced thinly
¼ cup (60ml) brandy

1 Preheat oven to 200°C/400°F. Grease four 1-cup (250ml) ovenproof dishes.
2 Peel and core pears; chop coarsely. Place pear in medium saucepan with sugar, cinnamon and the water; bring to the boil. Reduce heat; simmer, uncovered, about 10 minutes or until pears are tender. Strain pears over medium bowl; reserve syrup and cinnamon.
3 Cut eight 8.5cm (3½-inch) rounds from eight bread slices. Remove crusts from remaining bread slices; cut each slice into three 3cm (1¼-inch) wide strips. Halve each strip crossways.

4 Combine butter and 2 tablespoons of the reserved pear syrup in small bowl; brush butter mixture on one side of all bread pieces. Place one bread round, buttered-side down, in each dish; line side of each dish with bread fingers, buttered-side against dish, overlapping slightly. Fill centres with pear; top with remaining bread rounds, buttered-side up.
5 Bake charlottes about 30 minutes or until browned lightly.
6 Meanwhile, bring 1 cup of the reserved syrup and cinnamon to the boil in small saucepan; add figs. Reduce heat; simmer, uncovered, about 5 minutes or until syrup reduces by half. Add brandy; simmer, uncovered, 3 minutes.
7 Turn charlottes onto serving plates; spoon fig syrup over each charlotte.

QUEEN OF PUDDINGS

prep + cook time **55 minutes** makes **6**

2 cups (140g) stale breadcrumbs
1 tablespoon caster (superfine) sugar
1 teaspoon vanilla extract
1 teaspoon finely grated lemon rind
2½ cups (625ml) milk
60g (2 ounces) butter
4 eggs, separated
¼ cup (80g) raspberry jam, warmed
¾ cup (165g) caster (superfine) sugar, extra

1 Preheat oven to 180°C/350°F. Grease six ¾-cup (180ml) ovenproof dishes; place on oven tray.
2 Combine breadcrumbs, sugar, extract and rind in large bowl. Heat milk and butter in medium saucepan until almost boiling, pour over bread mixture; stand 10 minutes. Stir in egg yolks.
3 Divide mixture into dishes; bake about 30 minutes. Carefully spread top of hot puddings with jam.
4 Beat egg whites in small bowl with electric mixer until soft peaks form; gradually add extra sugar, beating until sugar dissolves. Spoon meringue over puddings; bake about 10 minutes.

queen of puddings

sticky date pudding with butterscotch sauce

STICKY DATE PUDDING WITH BUTTERSCOTCH SAUCE

prep + cook time **1 hour 40 minutes** serves **6**

1¾ cups (250g) coarsely chopped seeded
    dried dates
1¼ cups (310ml) water
1 teaspoon bicarbonate of soda
    (baking soda)
60g (2 ounces) butter
¾ cup (165g) caster (superfine) sugar
2 eggs
1 cup (150g) self-raising flour
butterscotch sauce
1 cup (220g) firmly packed light brown sugar
1 cup (250ml) pouring cream
200g (6½ ounces) butter

1 Preheat oven to 180°C/350°F. Grease deep 20cm (8-inch) round cake pan; line base with baking paper.
2 Combine dates and the water in medium saucepan; bring to the boil. Remove from heat, add soda; stand 5 minutes. Blend or process mixture until smooth.
3 Beat butter, sugar and one of the eggs in small bowl with electric mixer until light and fluffy. Beat in remaining egg (mixture will curdle at this stage, but will come together later). Stir in sifted flour then date mixture.
4 Pour mixture into pan; bake about 55 minutes. Stand pudding 10 minutes before turning onto wire rack over oven tray; turn pudding top-side up.
5 Meanwhile, make butterscotch sauce.
6 Pour ¼ cup sauce over pudding. Return pudding to moderate oven; bake, uncovered, further 5 minutes. Serve pudding with remaining sauce.
butterscotch sauce Stir ingredients in medium saucepan over heat, without boiling, until sugar dissolves. Reduce heat; simmer, uncovered, 3 minutes.

tip **This pudding can be made four days ahead; keep, covered, in refrigerator. Reheat single servings in microwave oven on HIGH (100%) for about 30 seconds just before serving.**

lemon delicious puddings

LEMON DELICIOUS PUDDINGS

prep + cook time **1 hour** makes **6**

125g (4 ounces) butter, melted
2 teaspoons finely grated lemon rind
1½ cups (330g) caster (superfine) sugar
3 eggs, separated
½ cup (75g) self-raising flour
⅓ cup (80ml) lemon juice
1⅓ cups (330ml) milk

1 Preheat oven to 180°C/350°F. Grease six 1-cup (250ml) ovenproof dishes.
2 Combine butter, rind, sugar and egg yolks in large bowl. Stir in sifted flour then juice. Gradually stir in milk; mixture should be smooth and runny.
3 Beat egg whites in small bowl with electric mixer until soft peaks form; fold into lemon mixture, in two batches.
4 Place ovenproof dishes in large baking dish; divide lemon mixture into dishes. Add enough boiling water to baking dish to come halfway up sides of ovenproof dishes.
5 Bake pudding about 45 minutes.

coffee and pecan puddings with caramel sauce

4 Spoon 2 tablespoons of the sauce over nuts in each mould; reserve remaining sauce.
5 Beat softened butter, extract and caster sugar in small bowl with electric mixer until light and fluffy. Beat in eggs, one at a time. Stir in sifted flours, milk and coffee; divide mixture into moulds.
6 Bake puddings about 30 minutes. Stand puddings 5 minutes before turning onto serving plates. Serve puddings with warm sauce.

tips **It's fine to use one 300ml carton of cream for this recipe. The caramel sauce and puddings can be made several hours ahead and reheated before serving.**

COFFEE AND PECAN PUDDINGS WITH CARAMEL SAUCE

prep + cook time **50 minutes** makes **6**

¾ cup (90g) coarsely chopped roasted pecans
1¼ cups (310ml) pouring cream
1½ cups (330g) firmly packed light brown sugar
100g (3 ounces) cold butter, chopped
125g (4 ounces) butter, softened
1 teaspoon vanilla extract
½ cup (110g) caster (superfine) sugar
2 eggs
1 cup (150g) self-raising flour
¼ cup (35g) plain (all-purpose) flour
¼ cup (60ml) milk
1 tablespoon finely ground espresso coffee

1 Preheat oven to 180°C/350°F. Grease six ¾-cup (180ml) metal moulds or ovenproof dishes; line bases with baking paper.
2 Divide nuts among moulds; place moulds on oven tray.
3 Stir cream, brown sugar and chopped butter in small saucepan over heat, without boiling, until sugar dissolves. Reduce heat; simmer, uncovered, without stirring, about 5 minutes or until mixture thickens slightly.

RHUBARB AND PEAR SPONGE PUDDING

prep + cook time **1 hour 10 minutes** serves **6**

825g (1¾ pounds) canned pear slices in natural juice
800g (1½ pounds) rhubarb, trimmed, cut into 4cm (1½-inch) pieces
2 tablespoons caster (superfine) sugar
2 eggs
⅓ cup (75g) caster (superfine) sugar, extra
2 tablespoons plain (all-purpose) flour
2 tablespoons self-raising flour
2 tablespoons cornflour (cornstarch)

1 Preheat oven to 180°C/350°F.
2 Drain pears; reserve ¾ cup of the juice.
3 Place reserved juice, rhubarb and sugar in large saucepan; cook, stirring occasionally, about 5 minutes or until rhubarb is just tender. Stir in pears. Pour mixture into deep 1.75-litre (7-cup) ovenproof dish.
4 Meanwhile, beat eggs in small bowl with electric mixer until thick and creamy. Gradually add extra sugar, beating until sugar dissolves. Fold in combined sifted flours.
5 Spread sponge mixture over hot rhubarb mixture. Bake pudding about 45 minutes or until browned lightly and cooked through.

rhubarb and pear sponge pudding

dark chocolate, raspberry and brioche pudding

DARK CHOCOLATE, RASPBERRY AND BRIOCHE PUDDING

prep + cook time **1 hour 10 minutes** serves **6**

40g (1½ ounces) butter, softened
300g (9½ ounces) brioche, sliced thickly
¼ cup (80g) raspberry jam
¾ cup (135g) coarsely grated dark eating
  (semi-sweet) chocolate
3 eggs
¼ cup (55g) caster (superfine) sugar
2½ cups (625ml) milk, heated
½ cup (75g) frozen raspberries

1 Preheat oven to 180°C/350°F. Grease shallow 2-litre (8-cup) ovenproof dish.
2 Butter one side of each brioche slice; spread unbuttered side with jam, sprinkle with chocolate.
3 Arrange brioche, butter-side up, overlapping slightly, in dish.
4 Whisk eggs, sugar and milk in large jug; pour over brioche, sprinkle with raspberries and any remaining chocolate.
5 Place dish in large baking dish; add enough boiling water to come halfway up side of dish.
6 Bake about 55 minutes or until pudding sets. Remove pudding from baking dish; stand 5 minutes before serving.

tip **Heating the milk before adding it to the pudding reduces its cooking time.**

ORANGE AND RASPBERRY SELF-SAUCING PUDDINGS

prep + cook time **20 minutes (+ standing)** serves **4**

¼ cup (20g) flaked almonds
30g (1 ounce) butter
¾ cup (110g) self-raising flour
⅓ cup (80ml) milk
⅔ cup (150g) firmly packed light brown sugar
2 teaspoons finely grated orange rind
¾ cup (110g) frozen raspberries
¼ cup (60ml) orange juice
¾ cup (180ml) boiling water

orange and raspberry self-saucing puddings

1 Grease shallow 1.5-litre (6-cup) microwave-safe dish.
2 Place nuts in small microwave-safe bowl; cook, uncovered, in microwave oven on HIGH (100%) about 2 minutes or until browned lightly.
3 Place butter in medium microwave-safe bowl; cook, uncovered, in microwave oven on HIGH (100%) 30 seconds. Add flour, milk and half of the sugar; whisk until smooth. Stir in rind and raspberries; spread mixture into dish.
4 Sprinkle remaining sugar over raspberry mixture; carefully pour over combined juice and the boiling water.
5 Place pudding on microwave-safe rack; cook, uncovered, in microwave oven on MEDIUM-HIGH (70%-80%) about 12 minutes. Stand 5 minutes. Sprinkle pudding with nuts. Serve with cream or ice-cream.

tips **If cooking in a conventional oven, grease 1.5-litre (6-cup) ovenproof dish. Bake, uncovered, in 200°C/400°F oven about 20 minutes. This recipe is best made close to serving.**

SUMMER PUDDING

prep + cook time **45 minutes (+ refrigeration)** serves **6**

3 eggs
½ cup (110g) caster (superfine) sugar
1 tablespoon cornflour (cornstarch)
¾ cup (110g) self-raising flour
1 teaspoon butter
¼ cup (60ml) boiling water
⅓ cup (75g) caster (superfine) sugar, extra
½ cup (125ml) water
2 cups (300g) frozen blackberries
3⅓ cups (500g) frozen mixed berries
¼ cup (80g) blackberry jam

1 Preheat oven to 180°C/350°F. Grease 23cm x 32cm (9-inch x 13-inch) swiss roll pan; line base and long sides with baking paper, extending paper 5cm (2 inches) over sides.
2 Beat eggs in small bowl with electric mixer until thick and creamy. Gradually add sugar, beating until sugar dissolves; transfer mixture to large bowl.
3 Fold triple-sifted flours into egg mixture. Pour combined butter and boiling water down side of bowl; fold into egg mixture. Spread mixture into pan; bake about 15 minutes. Cool in pan.
4 Meanwhile, combine extra sugar and the water in medium saucepan; bring to the boil. Stir in berries; return to the boil. Reduce heat; simmer, uncovered, until berries soften. Strain over medium bowl; reserve syrup and berries separately.

5 Turn cake onto board. Line 1.25-litre (5-cup) pudding basin with plastic wrap, extending wrap 10cm (4 inches) over side of basin. Cut circle slightly smaller than top edge of basin from cake using tip of sharp knife; cut second circle exact size of base of basin from cake. Cut remaining cake into 10cm (4-inch) long strips.
6 Place small cake circle in base of basin and use cake strips to line side of basin. Pour ⅔ cup of the reserved syrup into small jug; reserve. Fill basin with berries; cover with remaining syrup, top with large cake circle. Cover pudding with overhanging plastic wrap, weight pudding with saucer; refrigerate 3 hours or overnight.
7 Stir jam and 2 tablespoons of the reserved syrup in small saucepan until heated through. Turn pudding onto serving plate; brush with remaining reserved syrup then jam mixture. Serve with whipped cream.

rice pudding

RICE PUDDING

prep + cook time **1 hour 30 minutes** serves **6**

½ cup (100g) uncooked white
medium-grain rice
2½ cups (625ml) milk
¼ cup (55g) caster (superfine) sugar
¼ cup (40g) sultanas
½ teaspoon vanilla extract
2 teaspoons butter
½ teaspoon ground nutmeg

1 Preheat oven to 160°C/325°F. Grease
shallow 1-litre (4-cup) baking dish.
2 Wash rice under cold water; drain well.
Combine rice, milk, sugar, sultanas and extract
in dish; whisk lightly with fork. Dot with butter.
3 Bake, uncovered, 1 hour, whisking lightly
with fork under skin occasionally. Sprinkle with
nutmeg; bake 20 minutes. Serve warm or cold.

tip **Rice pudding can be stored, refrigerated, in an
airtight container for 2 days.**

MAPLE PECAN PUDDING

prep + cook time **1 hour** serves **10**

cooking-oil spray
1 cup (100g) pecans
⅓ cup (80ml) maple syrup
1¼ cups (235g) coarsely chopped dried figs
1¼ cups (310ml) boiling water
1 teaspoon bicarbonate of soda
(baking soda)
60g butter
¾ cup (150g) firmly packed light brown sugar
2 eggs
1 cup (150g) self-raising flour
maple butterscotch sauce
1 cup (250ml) maple syrup
½ cup (125ml) pouring cream
100g butter, chopped

maple pecan pudding

1 Preheat oven to 180°C/350°F. Grease deep
20cm (8-inch) round cake pan; line base with
baking paper. Spray paper with oil.
2 Arrange nuts over base of pan; drizzle with
maple syrup.
3 Place figs, the water and soda in bowl
of food processor. Cover with lid; stand
5 minutes. Add butter and sugar; process until
almost smooth. Add eggs and flour; process
until just combined. Pour mixture into pan.
4 Bake cake about 55 minutes. Stand cake
5 minutes; turn onto wire rack to cool.
5 Meanwhile, make maple butterscotch sauce.
6 Serve cake with sauce and vanilla ice-cream.
maple butterscotch sauce Stir ingredients in
small saucepan over heat until smooth; bring to
the boil. Boil, uncovered, about 2 minutes or
until mixture thickens slightly.

tip **You can use either pure maple syrup or
maple-flavoured syrup in this recipe.**

spiced crème caramel

3 Whisk eggs and extra sugar in medium bowl; whisking constantly, pour hot milk mixture into egg mixture. Strain mixture into cake pan; discard solids.
4 Meanwhile, preheat oven to 160°C/325°F.
5 Place pan in medium baking dish; add enough boiling water to come halfway up side of pan. Bake crème caramel about 40 minutes or until set. Remove pan from baking dish. Cover crème caramel; refrigerate overnight.
6 Gently ease crème caramel from side of pan; invert onto deep-sided serving plate.

tip It's fine to use one 300ml carton of cream for this recipe.

SPICED CREME CARAMEL

prep + cook time 1 hour (+ standing and refrigeration)
serves 6

¾ cup (165g) caster (superfine) sugar
½ cup (125ml) water
1¼ cups (310ml) pouring cream
1¾ cups (430ml) milk
4 cardamom pods, bruised
¼ teaspoon saffron threads
2 teaspoons rosewater
6 eggs
⅓ cup (75g) caster (superfine) sugar, extra

1 Stir sugar and the water in medium frying pan over heat, without boiling, until sugar dissolves; bring to the boil. Boil, uncovered, without stirring, until mixture is a dark caramel colour. Remove from heat; allow bubbles to subside. Pour toffee into deep 20cm (8-inch) round cake pan.
2 Combine cream, milk, spices and rosewater in medium saucepan; bring to the boil. Remove from heat; stand 30 minutes, then return to the boil.

BREAD AND BUTTER PUDDING

prep + cook time 1 hour 15 minutes serves 6

6 slices white bread (270g)
40g (1½ ounces) butter, softened
½ cup (80g) sultanas
¼ teaspoon ground nutmeg
custard
1½ cups (375ml) milk
2 cups (500ml) pouring cream
⅓ cup (75g) caster (superfine) sugar
1 teaspoon vanilla extract
4 eggs

1 Preheat oven to 160°C/325°F. Grease shallow 2-litre (8-cup) ovenproof dish.
2 Make custard.
3 Trim crusts from bread. Spread each slice with butter; cut into four triangles. Layer bread, overlapping, in dish; sprinkle with sultanas. Pour custard over bread; sprinkle with nutmeg.
4 Place ovenproof dish in large baking dish; add enough boiling water to come halfway up side of ovenproof dish. Bake about 45 minutes or until pudding sets. Remove pudding from baking dish; stand 5 minutes before serving. Serve dusted with sifted icing (confectioners') sugar, if you like.
custard Combine milk, cream, sugar and extract in medium saucepan; bring to the boil. Whisk eggs in large bowl; whisking constantly, gradually add hot milk mixture to egg mixture.

bread and butter pudding

plum clafoutis

PLUM CLAFOUTIS

prep + cook time **1 hour (+ cooling)** serves **6**

10 small plums (750g), halved, seeded
1 cinnamon stick, halved
¼ cup (60ml) water
¼ cup (55g) firmly packed light brown sugar
⅔ cup (160ml) milk
⅔ cup (160ml) pouring cream
1 teaspoon vanilla extract
4 eggs
½ cup (110g) caster (superfine) sugar
¼ cup (35g) plain (all-purpose) flour

1 Preheat oven to 200°C/400°F. Grease shallow 2.5-litre (10-cup) ovenproof dish.
2 Place plums in medium baking dish with cinnamon and the water; sprinkle with brown sugar. Roast about 15 minutes or until plums soften.
3 Remove cinnamon from dish and add to medium saucepan with milk, cream and extract; bring to the boil. Cool; remove cinnamon stick.
4 Whisk eggs and caster sugar in medium bowl until light and frothy; whisk in flour then whisk mixture into cream mixture.
5 Place drained plums in shallow ovenproof dish; pour cream mixture over plums.
6 Bake clafoutis about 30 minutes or until browned lightly. Serve dusted with sifted icing (confectioners') sugar.

tip **If plums are not in season, use a 1kg (2-pound) jar of whole plums. Drain, halve and seed them before using.**

PASSIONFRUIT SOUFFLES

prep + cook time **25 minutes** makes **4**

10g (½ ounce) butter, softened
1 tablespoon caster (superfine) sugar
2 eggs, separated
170g (5½ ounces) canned passionfruit in syrup
⅔ cup (110g) icing (confectioners') sugar
4 egg whites
1 tablespoon icing (confectioners') sugar, extra

passionfruit soufflés

1 Preheat oven to 220°C/425°F. Grease four 1-cup (250ml) soufflé dishes with butter; sprinkle with caster sugar, shake away excess.
2 Combine egg yolks, passionfruit and half the sifted icing sugar in large bowl.
3 Beat egg whites in small bowl with electric mixer until soft peaks form; add remaining sifted icing sugar, beat until firm peaks form. Gently fold a third of the egg white mixture into passionfruit mixture, then fold in remaining egg white mixture.
4 Place dishes on oven tray. Spoon soufflé mixture into dishes; bake about 12 minutes or until soufflés are puffed and golden. Dust with sifted extra icing sugar; serve immediately.

tip **The word soufflé is derived from the French verb "souffler", which means "to blow up" – when you see your soufflés magically rise in the oven, you'll understand exactly why it has the name it does.**

chocolate rum mini mousse

PASSIONFRUIT AND COCONUT CREME BRULEE

prep + cook time **1 hour (+ refrigeration)** makes **8**

2 eggs
4 egg yolks
¼ cup (55g) caster (superfine) sugar
½ cup (125ml) passionfruit pulp
1⅔ cups (400ml) coconut cream
1¼ cups (310ml) thickened (heavy) cream
2 tablespoons light brown sugar

1 Preheat oven to 180°C/350°F.
2 Combine eggs, egg yolks, caster sugar and passionfruit in medium heatproof bowl.
3 Bring coconut cream and cream to the boil in small saucepan. Gradually whisk hot cream mixture into egg mixture. Place bowl over medium saucepan of simmering water; stir over heat about 10 minutes or until custard mixture thickens slightly and coats the back of a spoon.
4 Divide custard into eight ½-cup (125ml) heatproof dishes or cups. Place dishes in large baking dish. Pour enough boiling water into baking dish to come halfway up sides of dishes.
5 Bake custards about 20 minutes or until custards just set. Remove custards from water; cool to room temperature. Cover; refrigerate 3 hours or overnight.
6 Preheat grill (broiler). Place custards in shallow flameproof dish filled with ice cubes. Sprinkle each custard with 1 teaspoon brown sugar; using finger, gently smooth over the surface of each custard. Place dish under grill until sugar caramelises.

tip **You will need about six passionfruit for this recipe.**

CHOCOLATE RUM MINI MOUSSE

prep + cook time **15 minutes** serves **4**

6 egg yolks
⅓ cup (75g) caster (superfine) sugar
½ cup (125ml) dark rum, warmed
50g (1½ ounces) dark eating (semi-sweet) chocolate, grated finely

1 Beat egg yolks and sugar in small deep-sided heatproof bowl with electric mixer until light and fluffy.
2 Place bowl over small saucepan of simmering water; whisk egg mixture constantly while gradually adding rum. Continue to whisk until mixture is thick and creamy. Add chocolate, in two batches, whisking gently until chocolate melts between additions.
3 Pour mousse mixture into four ⅓-cup (80ml) serving glasses.

tips **The mousse can be served chilled if desired; refrigerate about 2 hours. A variation on Italian zabaglione, the rum and chocolate transform this into a dessert of great depth and contrasting flavours. We used a caribbean rum for this recipe, for its mild smooth taste. Serve with almond biscotti or almond bread.**

passionfruit and coconut crème brûlée

saffron panna cotta with honeyed figs

SAFFRON PANNA COTTA WITH HONEYED FIGS

prep + cook time **30 minutes (+ refrigeration)** serves **6**

1 cup (250ml) pouring cream
½ cup (110g) caster (superfine) sugar
pinch saffron threads
8 cardamom pods, bruised
2 cinnamon sticks
4 teaspoons gelatine
2 tablespoons water
2 cups (500ml) buttermilk
honeyed figs
¼ cup (90g) honey
¼ cup (60ml) dry red wine
⅓ cup (65g) finely chopped dried figs

1 Stir cream, sugar and spices in medium saucepan over low heat until sugar dissolves; bring to the boil. Strain mixture into large heatproof jug; cool 5 minutes.
2 Meanwhile, sprinkle gelatine over the water in small heatproof jug. Stand jug in small saucepan of simmering water; stir until gelatine dissolves, cool 5 minutes.
3 Stir gelatine mixture and buttermilk into cream mixture. Divide mixture into six ¾-cup (180ml) moulds. Cover; refrigerate 4 hours or until set.
4 Make honeyed figs.
5 Turn panna cottas onto serving plates; top with honeyed figs.
honeyed figs Combine ingredients in medium saucepan; bring to the boil. Reduce heat; simmer, uncovered, about 5 minutes or until syrup thickens slightly. Cool.

ice-cream puddings with rocky road sauce

ICE-CREAM PUDDINGS WITH ROCKY ROAD SAUCE

prep + cook time **30 minutes** makes **4**

1 litre (4 cups) vanilla ice-cream, softened
2 x 60g (2-ounce) Snickers bars,
chopped finely
2 x 50g (1½-ounce) Crunchie bars,
chopped finely
⅔ cup (160ml) thickened (heavy) cream
100g (3 ounces) dark eating (semi-sweet)
chocolate, chopped coarsely
100g (3 ounces) rocky road,
chopped coarsely

1 Line four 1-cup (250ml) metal moulds with plastic wrap.
2 Place ice-cream in large bowl; fold in chocolate bars. Divide mixture into prepared moulds. Cover with foil; freeze about 15 minutes or until firm.
3 Meanwhile, heat cream and chocolate in small saucepan over low heat, stirring until smooth. Remove from heat; stir rocky road into sauce mixture.
4 Turn ice-cream timbales onto serving plates; drizzle with rocky road sauce.

PEACH AND AMARETTI CRUMBLES

prep + cook time **35 minutes** serves **4**

Preheat oven to 200°C/400°F. Grease four 1¼-cup (310ml) ovenproof dishes; place on oven tray. Cook 4 thickly sliced large peaches, 2 tablespoons caster (superfine) sugar and ½ teaspoon mixed spice in medium saucepan, stirring, over medium heat, until peaches are tender; divide mixture into dishes. Meanwhile, combine 125g (4 ounces) crushed amaretti biscuits, ¼ cup ground almonds and ¼ cup plain (all-purpose) flour in medium bowl; rub in 80g (2½ ounces) chopped butter then sprinkle mixture evenly over peaches. Bake crumbles about 20 minutes or until browned.

BERRY AND HAZELNUT CRUMBLES

prep + cook time **30 minutes** serves **4**

Preheat oven to 220°C/425°F. Grease four shallow ¾-cup (180ml) ovenproof dishes; place on oven tray. Combine 300g (9½ ounces) frozen mixed berries, 1 tablespoon lemon juice, 1 tablespoon light brown sugar and ¼ cup finely chopped roasted hazelnuts in medium bowl; divide mixture into dishes. Blend or process 1 tablespoon light brown sugar, ¼ cup finely chopped roasted hazelnuts, 2 tablespoons plain (all-purpose) flour and 20g (¾ ounce) cold butter until ingredients come together; stir in ¼ cup rolled oats. Sprinkle over berry mixture. Bake crumbles about 20 minutes or until browned lightly.

CRUMBLES

APRICOTS WITH CRUMBLE TOPPING

prep + cook time **25 minutes** serves **4**

Preheat oven to 200°C/400°F. Halve 4 large fresh apricots; remove stones. Place apricots, cut-side up, on oven tray. Combine ½ cup rolled oats, 2 tablespoons finely chopped dried apricots, 1 tablespoon light brown sugar, 1 tablespoon honey and 1 tablespoon warm water in small bowl; spoon mixture onto apricot halves. Bake about 15 minutes or until fruit is tender. Meanwhile, combine ⅓ cup smooth reduced-fat ricotta cheese, ¼ teaspoon ground cinnamon and a pinch ground cardamom in small bowl. Serve fruit with spiced ricotta.

APPLE AND RASPBERRY CRUMBLES

prep + cook time **35 minutes** serves **4**

Preheat oven to 220°C/425°F. Cook 4 coarsely chopped medium green apples, 2 teaspoons finely grated lemon rind, ¼ cup lemon juice and ¼ cup firmly packed light brown sugar in large frying pan until apples begin to caramelise. Stir in 2 teaspoons mixed spice, 2 tablespoons water and 500g (1 pound) frozen raspberries. Divide mixture into four 1-cup (250ml) shallow ovenproof dishes; top with 125g (4 ounces) crumbled scotch finger biscuits. Place dishes on oven tray. Bake crumbles about 10 minutes or until browned.

CHOC-CHERRY TRIFLES

prep + cook time **15 minutes** makes **4**

Combine 300g (9½ ounces) thawed frozen pitted black cherries and ⅓ cup marsala in small bowl. Reserve 8 biscotti from 170g (5½ ounces) chocolate hazelnut biscotti, then chop remaining biscotti coarsely. Place 6 x 62g (2-ounce) tubs chocolate mousse in medium bowl; whisk until smooth. Spoon half the cherry mixture into four 2-cup (500ml) serving glasses; top with half the chopped biscotti and half the mousse. Repeat layering. Serve trifles with reserved biscotti.

BERRY TRIFLE

prep + cook time **30 minutes (+ refrigeration)** serves **6**

Combine 1 tablespoon custard powder with 2 teaspoons white (granulated) sugar and 1 cup milk in small saucepan; stir over low heat until custard boils and thickens. Beat 1¼ cups (310ml) thickened (heavy) cream, 2 teaspoons icing (confectioners') sugar and 1 teaspoon vanilla extract in small bowl with electric mixer until soft peaks form. Dip 12 sponge-finger biscuits, one at a time, in 1 cup apple juice; cover base of 1.5-litre (6-cup) serving dish with some of the biscuits. Top with custard and 150g (4½ ounces) frozen mixed berries. Top with remaining dipped biscuits, cream and 150g (4½ ounces) frozen mixed berries. Refrigerate 2 hours.

tip **It's fine to use one 300ml carton of cream for this recipe.**

PAVLOVA TRIFLES

prep + cook time **25 minutes** makes **4**

Beat ¾ cup thickened (heavy) cream and
2 tablespoons icing (confectioners') sugar in
small bowl with electric mixer until soft peaks
form; stir in 200g (6½ ounces) crème fraîche.
Divide 250g (8 ounces) quartered strawberries
and 2 thickly sliced medium bananas into four
1½-cup (375ml) glasses. Top with ¼ cup
passionfruit pulp. Divide crème fraîche mixture
into glasses; top with 50g (1½ ounces) coarsely
chopped meringues, 3 coarsely chopped
medium kiwi fruit and ¼ cup passionfruit pulp.

tips You need 6 passionfruit to get the required amount
of pulp for this recipe. Packaged pavlova "nests" and
meringues can be found at your supermarket.

LAST-MINUTE TRIFLES

prep time **25 minutes** makes **6**

Divide a coarsely chopped 125g (4-ounce)
sponge cake into six ¾-cup (180ml) serving
glasses; drizzle ¼ cup sweet sherry over the
sponge. Whip 1¼ cups (310ml) thickened
(heavy) cream until soft peaks form. Thinly slice
125g (4 ounces) strawberries. Coarsely chop
3 x 155g (5-ounce) raspberry-flavoured jelly
(jello) cups. Top sponge with ½ cup thick
custard, jelly, the cream, then the strawberries.

tip It's fine to use one 300ml carton of cream for this recipe.

QUINCE AND RHUBARB PIE

prep + cook time 3 hours (+ refrigeration) **serves** 8

2 cups (500ml) water
2 cups (440g) caster (superfine) sugar
4 medium quinces (1.2kg), peeled, quartered
2 strips lemon rind
500g (1 pound) rhubarb, chopped coarsely
¼ cup (60ml) lemon juice, approximately
1 cup (150g) plain (all-purpose) flour
⅓ cup (55g) icing (confectioners') sugar
100g (3 ounces) cold butter, chopped
1 egg, separated
1 tablespoon iced water, approximately
1 tablespoon raw sugar

1 Stir the water and sugar in medium saucepan over low heat until sugar dissolves. Add quince and rind; bring to the boil. Reduce heat; simmer, covered, about 2 hours, or until quinces are tender and a rosy colour. Add rhubarb; cook 5 minutes or until rhubarb softens. Add juice to taste, to reduce sweetness. Cool quince and rhubarb in the syrup.
2 Meanwhile, process flour, icing sugar and butter until crumbly. Add egg yolk and iced water, process until ingredients come together. Knead dough on floured surface until smooth. Cover; refrigerate 30 minutes.
3 Preheat oven to 180°C/350°F. Grease 24cm (9½-inch) pie dish.
4 Drain fruit mixture, reserving ⅓ cup of the syrup. Spoon fruit mixture and reserved syrup into dish.
5 Roll out pastry until large enough to cover pie. Using a 1cm (½-inch) cutter, cut out rounds from pastry, reserving rounds. Place pastry over filling, trim edge with a knife. Place rounds on pastry, brush a little of the lightly beaten egg white over pastry; sprinkle with raw sugar. Place pie on an oven tray.
6 Bake pie about 30 minutes or until well browned. (Cover the edges of the pastry with foil after 20 minutes to prevent over-browning). Stand 10 minutes before serving with thick (double) cream, if you like.

PIES

LEMON CHIFFON PIE

prep + cook time **40 minutes (+ refrigeration & standing)**
serves **8**

1¾ cups (180g) plain sweet biscuit crumbs
125g (4 ounces) butter, melted
filling
4 eggs, separated
⅓ cup (75g) caster (superfine) sugar
3 teaspoons gelatine
2 teaspoons grated lemon rind
⅓ cup (80ml) lemon juice
⅓ cup (80ml) water
⅓ cup (75g) caster (superfine) sugar, extra

1 Combine biscuit crumbs and butter in medium bowl. Press mixture firmly over base and side of 24cm (9½-inch) pie dish; refrigerate 30 minutes or until firm.

2 Meanwhile, make filling.

3 Spread filling into crumb crust; refrigerate several hours or until set.

filling Stir egg yolks, sugar, gelatine, rind, juice and the water in medium heatproof bowl over medium saucepan of simmering water until mixture has thickened slightly. Remove from heat; pour into large bowl. Cover; cool to room temperature. Mixture should be set to about the consistency of unbeaten egg white before remaining ingredients are added. Beat egg whites in small bowl with electric mixer until soft peaks form; gradually add extra sugar, beating until sugar dissolves. Fold egg white mixture into lemon mixture, in two batches.

TREACLE TART

prep + cook time **1 hour (+ refrigeration & standing)**
serves **8**

1¼ cups (185g) plain (all-purpose) flour
⅓ cup (40g) custard powder
2 tablespoons icing (confectioners') sugar
125g (4 ounces) butter, chopped
2 tablespoons milk, approximately
filling
1½ cups (100g) stale breadcrumbs
1 cup (360g) treacle
2 teaspoons grated lemon rind

1 Sift flour, custard powder and icing sugar into medium bowl; rub in butter. Add enough milk to make ingredients come together. Knead dough on floured surface until smooth. Cover; refrigerate 30 minutes.
2 Preheat oven to 200°C/400°F.
3 Roll two-thirds of the dough between sheets of baking paper until large enough to line 24cm (9½-inch) round loose-based fluted flan tin. Ease pastry into tin, press into base and side; trim edge. Place tin on oven tray. Line pastry case with baking paper; fill with dried beans or rice. Bake 10 minutes; remove paper and beans. Bake further 10 minutes or until browned lightly. Cool.
4 Reduce oven to 180°C/350°F.
5 Make filling; spread into pastry case.
6 Roll remaining pastry into a rectangle on floured surface; cut into 1cm (½-inch) strips. Brush edge of pastry case with a little extra milk. Place pastry strips over filling in lattice pattern; brush pastry with a little more milk.
7 Bake tart about 25 minutes or until pastry is browned lightly. Cool tart in tin. Just before serving, dust with icing (confectioners') sugar, if you like. Serve with whipped cream or ice-cream.
filling Combine ingredients in medium bowl.

COUNTRY APPLE PIE

prep + cook time **1 hour (+ refrigeration)** serves **6**

1¾ cups (260g) plain (all-purpose) flour
¼ cup (35g) self-raising flour
1 tablespoon icing (confectioners') sugar
125g (4 ounces) butter, chopped
1 egg, beaten lightly
2 tablespoons lemon juice, approximately
1 egg white
2 tablespoons apricot jam
apple filling
5 large apples (1kg), sliced thinly
¼ cup (60ml) water
2 tablespoons caster (superfine) sugar
1 teaspoon grated lemon rind

1 Sift flours and sugar into medium bowl; rub in butter. Add egg and enough juice to make ingredients come together. Knead dough on floured surface until smooth. Cover; refrigerate 30 minutes.

2 Meanwhile, make apple filling.

3 Grease 24cm (9½-inch) round loose-based fluted flan tin. Roll three-quarters of the pastry between sheets of baking paper until large enough to line tin. Ease pastry into tin, press into base and side; trim edge. Cover; refrigerate 30 minutes, along with remaining pastry and any scraps.

4 Preheat oven to 200°C/400°F.

5 Line pastry case with baking paper; fill with dried beans or rice. Bake 7 minutes; remove paper and beans. Bake further 7 minutes.

6 Spread cold apple filling into pastry case. Roll remaining pastry out to 3mm (⅛-inch) thickness, cut into 1cm (½-inch) strips. Brush edge of pastry with egg white. Place pastry strips over filling in a lattice pattern, press gently against edge of pastry, brush with egg white.

7 Bake pie about 20 minutes or until pastry is golden brown. Brush pie with warmed sieved jam.

apple filling Bring apples and the water to the boil in large saucepan. Reduce heat; simmer, covered, over low heat about 5 minutes or until apples are tender. Stir in sugar and rind; cool, drain.

lemon meringue pie

LEMON MERINGUE PIE

prep + cook time **1 hour (+ refrigeration)** serves **10**

½ cup (75g) cornflour (cornstarch)
1 cup (220g) caster (superfine) sugar
½ cup (125ml) lemon juice
1¼ cups (310ml) water
2 teaspoons finely grated lemon rind
60g (2 ounces) unsalted butter, chopped
3 eggs, separated
½ cup (110g) caster (superfine) sugar, extra
pastry
1½ cups (225g) plain (all-purpose) flour
1 tablespoon icing (confectioners') sugar
140g (4½ ounces) cold butter, chopped
1 egg yolk
2 tablespoons cold water

1 Make pastry.
2 Grease 24cm (9½-inch) round loose-based fluted flan tin. Roll pastry between sheets of baking paper until large enough to line tin. Ease pastry into tin, press into base and side; trim edge. Cover; refrigerate 30 minutes.
3 Preheat oven to 240°C/425°F.
4 Place tin on oven tray. Line pastry case with baking paper; fill with dried beans or rice. Bake 15 minutes; remove paper and beans. Bake further 10 minutes; cool pastry case, turn oven off.
5 Meanwhile, combine cornflour and sugar in medium saucepan; gradually stir in juice and the water until smooth. Cook, stirring, over high heat, until mixture boils and thickens. Reduce heat; simmer, stirring, 1 minute. Remove from heat; stir in rind, butter and egg yolks. Cool 10 minutes.
6 Spread filling into pastry case. Cover; refrigerate 2 hours.
7 Preheat oven to 240°C/475°F.
8 Beat egg whites in small bowl with electric mixer until soft peaks form; gradually add extra sugar, beating until sugar dissolves.
9 Roughen surface of filling with fork before spreading with meringue mixture. Bake about 2 minutes or until browned lightly.
pastry Process flour, icing sugar and butter until crumbly. Add egg yolk and the water; process until ingredients come together. Knead dough on floured surface until smooth. Cover; refrigerate 30 minutes.

apple cinnamon tarts

APPLE CINNAMON TARTS

prep + cook time **30 minutes** serves **4**

1 large golden delicious apple (200g)
1 sheet sweet puff pastry
20g (¾ ounce) butter, melted
1 teaspoon cinnamon sugar
¼ cup (80g) apricot jam, warmed

1 Preheat oven to 220°C/425°F. Grease oven tray.
2 Peel, core and halve apple; slice thinly.
3 Cut pastry sheet in half to form two rectangles; place on tray. Overlap apple slices down centre of pastry halves. Brush apple with butter; sprinkle with cinnamon sugar.
4 Bake tarts about 15 minutes or until pastry is browned. Brush tarts with jam.

peanut butter ice-cream pie

PEANUT BUTTER ICE-CREAM PIE

prep + cook time **30 minutes (+ freezing)** serves **10**

300g (9½ ounces) chocolate chip cookies
40g (1½ ounces) butter, melted
1 tablespoon milk
1 litre (4 cups) vanilla ice-cream, softened
1⅓ cups (375g) crunchy peanut butter
hot fudge sauce
200g (6½ ounces) dark eating (semi-sweet)
**   chocolate, chopped coarsely**
50g (1½ ounces) white marshmallows,
**   chopped coarsely**
1¼ cups (310ml) thickened (heavy) cream

1 Grease 24cm (9½-inch) round loose-based fluted flan tin.
2 Blend or process cookies until mixture resembles coarse breadcrumbs. Add butter and milk; process until combined.
3 Press cookie mixture over base and side of tin; refrigerate 10 minutes.
4 Beat softened ice-cream and peanut butter in large bowl with electric mixer until combined. Spoon pie filling into crumb crust. Cover; freeze pie 3 hours or overnight.
5 Make hot fudge sauce.

6 Serve pie, drizzled with fudge sauce.
hot fudge sauce Stir ingredients in small saucepan over heat, without boiling, until smooth.

tip **It's fine to use one 300ml carton of cream for this recipe.**

BANOFFEE PIE

prep + cook time **1 hour (+ refrigeration)** serves **8**

395g (12½ ounces) canned sweetened
**   condensed milk**
75g (2½ ounces) butter, chopped
½ cup (110g) firmly packed light brown sugar
2 tablespoons golden syrup (or treacle)
2 large bananas (460g), sliced thinly
1¼ cups (310ml) thickened (heavy) cream,
**   whipped**
pastry
1½ cups (225g) plain (all-purpose) flour
1 tablespoon icing (confectioners') sugar
140g (4½ ounces) cold butter, chopped
1 egg yolk
2 tablespoons cold water

1 Make pastry.
2 Grease 24cm (9½-inch) round loose-based fluted flan tin. Roll pastry between sheets of baking paper until large enough to line tin. Ease pastry into tin, press into base and side; trim edge. Prick base all over with fork. Cover; refrigerate 30 minutes.
3 Preheat oven to 200°C/400°F.
4 Place tin on oven tray; line pastry with baking paper, fill with dried beans or rice. Bake 10 minutes; remove paper and beans. Bake further 10 minutes; cool.
5 Meanwhile, cook condensed milk, butter, sugar and syrup in medium saucepan over medium heat, stirring, about 10 minutes or until mixture is caramel-coloured. Stand 5 minutes; pour into pastry case, cool.
6 Arrange banana slices on caramel; top with cream and a pinch of ground cinnamon, if you like.
pastry Process flour, sugar and butter until crumbly; add egg yolk and the water, process until ingredients come together. Knead dough on floured surface until smooth. Cover; refrigerate 30 minutes.

tip **It's fine to use one 300ml carton of cream for this recipe.**

banoffee pie

BLACK BOTTOM PIE

prep + cook time 1 hour (+ refrigeration) serves 8

90g (3 ounces) butter
¼ cup (55g) caster (superfine) sugar
1 egg
1 cup (150g) plain (all-purpose) flour
¼ cup (35g) self-raising flour
½ cup (125ml) thickened (heavy) cream,
  whipped
30g (1 ounce) dark eating (semi-sweet)
  chocolate, grated
filling
1 tablespoon gelatine
¼ cup (60ml) milk
¼ cup (55g) caster (superfine) sugar
3 teaspoons cornflour (cornstarch)
1 cup (250ml) milk, extra
3 eggs, separated
60g (2 ounces) dark eating (semi-sweet)
  chocolate, melted
1 teaspoon vanilla extract
¼ cup (55g) caster (superfine) sugar, extra

1 Beat butter and sugar in small bowl with electric mixer until just combined; beat in egg. Stir in sifted flours, in two batches. Turn dough onto floured surface; knead until smooth. Cover; refrigerate 30 minutes.
2 Meanwhile, make filling.
3 Preheat oven to 200°C/400°F. Roll pastry on floured surface until large enough to line 24cm (9½-inch) pie dish. Ease pastry into dish, press into base and side; trim edge. Prick pastry all over with fork.
4 Bake pastry case about 15 minutes or until browned; cool.
5 Spread chocolate custard into pastry case; refrigerate until firm. Spread vanilla custard into pastry case; refrigerate until firm. Spread whipped cream over custard, then sprinkle with grated chocolate.
filling Sprinkle gelatine over milk in small jug. Blend sugar and cornflour with extra milk in small saucepan; stir over heat until mixture boils and thickens, remove from heat. Quickly stir in egg yolks, then gelatine mixture; stir until smooth. Divide custard into two bowls. Stir chocolate into one bowl. Cover both bowls; cool to room temperature. Stir extract into plain custard. Beat egg whites in small bowl with electric mixer until soft peaks form; gradually add extra sugar, beating until dissolved after additions. Fold egg white mixture into vanilla custard, in two batches.

PISTACHIO ORANGE PIE

prep + cook time **1 hour 20 minutes (+ refrigeration)**
serves **10**

1⅓ cups (185g) coarsely chopped
    unsalted pistachios
1 tablespoon plain (all-purpose) flour
2 tablespoons light brown sugar
40g (1½ ounces) butter, melted
2 eggs
¾ cup (180ml) maple syrup
2 teaspoons finely grated orange rind
1 tablespoon orange juice
2 tablespoons orange marmalade,
    warmed, sieved
pastry
1¼ cups (185g) plain (all-purpose) flour
⅓ cup (55g) icing (confectioners') sugar
125g (4 ounces) cold butter, chopped coarsely
1 egg yolk
1 teaspoon iced water, approximately

1 Make pastry.
2 Grease 24cm (9½-inch) round loose-based fluted flan tin. Roll pastry between sheets of baking paper until large enough to line tin. Ease pastry into tin, press into base and side; trim edge. Cover; refrigerate 30 minutes.
3 Preheat oven to 180°C/350°F.
4 Place tin on oven tray. Line pastry case with baking paper; fill with dried beans or rice. Bake 10 minutes; remove paper and beans. Bake further 5 minutes; cool.
5 Reduce oven to 160°C/325°F.
6 Combine nuts, flour, sugar, butter, eggs, syrup, rind and juice in medium bowl. Pour mixture into pastry case.
7 Bake pie about 45 minutes. Cool. Brush pie with marmalade.
pastry Process flour, icing sugar and butter until crumbly. Add egg yolk and enough of the water to process until ingredients come together. Knead dough on floured surface until smooth. Cover; refrigerate 30 minutes.

SPICED APRICOT AND PLUM PIE

prep + cook time **1 hour (+ cooling)** serves **8**

**1.65kg (3¼ pounds) canned dark plums
in light syrup**
2 cups (300g) dried apricots
1 cinnamon stick
3 cloves
½ teaspoon mixed spice
½ teaspoon ground ginger
2 sheets puff pastry
1 egg, beaten lightly
spiced yogurt cream
½ cup (140g) yogurt
½ cup (120g) sour cream
1 tablespoon ground cinnamon
¼ teaspoon ground ginger
1 tablespoon icing (confectioners') sugar

1 Preheat oven to 200°C/400°F.
Grease 26cm (10½-inch) pie dish or deep
1.25-litre (5-cup) rectangular dish.
2 Drain plums; reserve 1 cup of the syrup.
Halve plums, discard stones, place plums
in dish.
3 Place reserved syrup, apricots, cinnamon,
cloves, mixed spice and ginger in medium
saucepan; simmer, uncovered, until liquid is
reduced to ½ cup. Remove and discard
cinnamon stick and cloves; cool to room
temperature. Pour mixture over plums.
4 Cut pastry into 2.5cm (1-inch) strips.
Brush edge of dish with some of the egg;
press pastry strips around edge of dish.
Twist remaining strips, place over filling in a lattice
pattern; trim ends, brush top with remaining egg.
5 Bake pie about 40 minutes or until
browned lightly.
6 Make spiced yogurt cream.
7 Dust pie with a little extra icing sugar if you
like, and serve with spiced yogurt cream.
spiced yogurt cream Combine ingredients in
small bowl.

BERRY AND RHUBARB PIES

prep + cook time **1 hour (+ refrigeration)** makes **6**

2 cups (220g) coarsely chopped rhubarb
¼ cup (55g) caster (superfine) sugar
2 tablespoons water
1 tablespoon cornflour (cornstarch)
2 cups (300g) frozen mixed berries
1 egg white
2 teaspoons caster (superfine) sugar, extra
pastry
1⅔ cups (250g) plain (all-purpose) flour
⅓ cup (75g) caster (superfine) sugar
150g (4½ ounces) cold butter,
    chopped coarsely
1 egg yolk

1 Make pastry.
2 Place rhubarb, sugar and half the water in medium saucepan; bring to the boil. Reduce heat; simmer, covered, about 3 minutes or until rhubarb is tender. Blend cornflour with the remaining water; stir into rhubarb mixture. Stir over heat until mixture boils and thickens. Remove from heat; stir in berries. Cool.
3 Grease six-hole (¾-cup/180ml) texas muffin pan. Roll two-thirds of the pastry between sheets of baking paper to 3mm (⅛-inch) thickness; cut out six 12cm (4¾-inch) rounds. Press rounds into pan holes. Refrigerate 30 minutes.
4 Preheat oven to 200°C/400°F.
5 Roll remaining pastry between sheets of baking paper to 3mm (⅛-inch) thickness; cut out six 9cm (3¾-inch) rounds.
6 Spoon fruit mixture into pastry cases.
7 Brush edge of 9cm (3¾-inch) rounds with egg white; place over filling. Press edges firmly to seal. Brush tops with egg white; sprinkle with extra sugar.
8 Bake pies about 30 minutes. Stand in pan 10 minutes; using palette knife, loosen pies from edge of pan before lifting out. Serve warm with vanilla ice-cream.
pastry Process flour, sugar and butter until crumbly. Add egg yolk; process until ingredients come together. Knead dough on floured surface until smooth. Cover; refrigerate 30 minutes.

tips **You need 4 large stems of rhubarb for this recipe. If pastry is too dry, add 2 teaspoons of water with the egg yolk.**

PUMPKIN PIE

prep + cook time **1 hour 15 minutes (+ refrigeration)**
serves **8**

1 cup (150g) plain (all-purpose) flour
¼ cup (35g) self-raising flour
2 tablespoons cornflour (cornstarch)
2 tablespoons icing (confectioners') sugar
125g (4 ounces) butter, chopped
2 tablespoons water, approximately
filling
2 eggs
¼ cup (55g) firmly packed light brown sugar
2 tablespoons maple syrup
1 cup cooked mashed pumpkin
⅔ cup (160ml) evaporated milk
1 teaspoon ground cinnamon
½ teaspoon ground nutmeg
pinch ground allspice

1 Sift flours and sugar into medium bowl; rub in butter. Add enough of the water to make ingredients come together. Knead dough on floured surface until smooth. Cover; refrigerate 30 minutes.

2 Preheat oven to 200°C/400°F.

3 Roll pastry on floured surface until large enough to line 24cm (9½-inch) pie dish. Ease pastry into dish, press into base and side; trim edge. Use scraps of pastry to make a double edge of pastry; trim and decorate edge.

4 Place pie dish on oven tray; line pastry case with baking paper; fill with dried beans or rice. Bake 10 minutes; remove paper and beans. Bake further 10 minutes or until browned lightly; cool.

5 Meanwhile, make filling.

6 Reduce oven to 180°C/350°F.

7 Pour filling into pastry case; bake about 50 minutes or until filling is set. Cool. Serve dusted with extra sifted icing sugar, if you like.

filling Beat eggs, sugar and maple syrup in small bowl with electric mixer until thick. Stir in pumpkin, milk and spices.

tip **You will need to cook about 350g (11 ounces) pumpkin for this recipe.**

baked passionfruit tart

BAKED PASSIONFRUIT TART

prep + cook time **1 hour 30 minutes (+ refrigeration
& standing)** serves 8

1½ cups (225g) plain (all-purpose) flour
⅓ cup (55g) icing (confectioners') sugar
150g (4½ ounces) cold unsalted
    butter, chopped
2 egg yolks
filling
7 egg yolks
1 cup (220g) caster (superfine) sugar
1 teaspoon finely grated lemon rind
⅓ cup (80ml) passionfruit pulp
1 cup (250ml) thickened (heavy) cream

1 Process flour, sugar and butter until crumbly.
Add egg yolks; process until ingredients come
together. Knead dough on floured surface until
smooth. Cover; refrigerate 30 minutes.
2 Roll pastry between sheets of baking paper
until large enough to line 24cm (9½-inch) round
loose-based fluted flan tin. Ease pastry into tin,
press into base and side; trim edge. Cover;
refrigerate 1 hour.
3 Preheat oven to 200°C/400°F.

4 Place tin on oven tray. Line pastry with
baking paper; fill with dried beans or rice.
Bake 10 minutes; remove paper and beans.
Bake further 10 minutes or until browned
lightly. Cool.
5 Reduce oven to 150°C/300°F.
6 Make filling; pour into pastry case.
7 Bake tart about 1 hour or until just set; cool.
Serve at room temperature, dusted with a little
sifted icing (confectioners') sugar.
filling Combine ingredients in medium bowl.

tip **You will need about 4 passionfruit for this recipe.**

CHOCOLATE ALMOND JALOUSIE

prep + cook time **1 hour (+ freezing)** serves 4

50g (1½ ounces) dark eating (semi-sweet)
    chocolate, chopped coarsely
¼ cup (55g) caster (superfine) sugar
1 tablespoon cocoa powder
½ cup (60g) ground almonds
20g (¾ ounce) cold unsalted butter,
    chopped finely
2 teaspoons brandy
2 eggs
2 sheets puff pastry

1 Process chocolate, sugar, cocoa and
ground almonds until chocolate is chopped
finely. Add butter; process until mixture begins
to come together. Add brandy and 1 egg;
process to combine.
2 Cut one pastry sheet into a 12cm x 24cm
(4¾-inch x 9½-inch) rectangle; cut the other
into a 14cm x 24cm (5½-inch x 9½-inch)
rectangle. Leaving a 2cm (¾-inch) border along
all sides, cut even slits in centre of larger pastry
sheet at 2cm (¾-inch) intervals. Place smaller
sheet on greased oven tray; spread centre
with chocolate mixture, leaving a 2cm (¾-inch)
border. Brush edges with a little of the remaining
beaten egg.
3 Top with other pastry sheet, press edges
together. Freeze 10 minutes.
4 Preheat oven to 200°C/400°F.
5 Brush pastry lightly with remaining
beaten egg; bake about 35 minutes or until
browned lightly.

chocolate almond jalousie

chocolate tart

CHOCOLATE TART

prep + cook time **1 hour 30 minutes** (+ refrigeration)
serves **8**

1½ cups (225g) plain (all-purpose) flour
½ cup (110g) caster (superfine) sugar
140g (4½ ounces) cold butter, chopped coarsely
1 egg, beaten lightly
1 teaspoon cocoa powder
chocolate filling
2 eggs
2 egg yolks
¼ cup (55g) caster (superfine) sugar
250g (8 ounces) dark eating (semi-sweet)
    chocolate, melted
200g (6½ ounces) butter, melted

1 Process flour, sugar and butter until crumbly.
Add egg; process until ingredients come
together. Knead dough on floured surface until
smooth. Cover; refrigerate 30 minutes.
2 Roll pastry between sheets of baking paper
until large enough to line greased 24cm (9½-inch)
round loose-based fluted flan tin. Ease pastry
into tin, press into base and side; trim edge,
prick base all over with fork. Cover; refrigerate
30 minutes.
3 Meanwhile, preheat oven to 200°C/400°F.
4 Make chocolate filling.
5 Place tin on oven tray. Line pastry with
baking paper; fill with dried beans or rice. Bake
10 minutes; remove paper and beans. Bake
further 5 minutes or until browned lightly. Cool.
6 Reduce oven to 180°C/350°F.
7 Pour chocolate filling into pastry case.
Bake about 10 minutes or until filling is set;
cool 10 minutes. Refrigerate 1 hour. Serve
dusted with sifted cocoa powder. Serve tart
topped with strawberries.
chocolate filling Whisk eggs, egg yolks and
sugar in medium heatproof bowl over medium
saucepan of simmering water (don't let water
touch base of bowl) about 15 minutes or until
light and fluffy. Remove from heat. Gently whisk
chocolate and butter into egg mixture.

impossible pie

IMPOSSIBLE PIE

prep + cook time **55 minutes** serves **8**

½ cup (75g) plain (all-purpose) flour
1 cup (220g) caster (superfine) sugar
¾ cup (60g) desiccated coconut
4 eggs
1 teaspoon vanilla extract
125g (4 ounces) butter, melted
½ cup (40g) flaked almonds
2 cups (500ml) milk

1 Preheat oven to 180°C/350°F. Grease deep
24cm (9½-inch) pie dish.
2 Combine sifted flour, sugar, coconut, eggs,
extract, butter and half the nuts in large bowl;
gradually add milk, stirring, until combined.
Pour mixture into dish.
3 Bake pie 35 minutes. Remove pie from oven,
sprinkle top with remaining nuts; bake further
10 minutes. Serve with cream, if you like.

tip **When you make this pie you will discover how it got
its name; when cooked, the pie magically separates into
three perfect layers. Impossible!**

portuguese custard tarts

SPICED STONE FRUIT STRUDEL

prep + cook time **45 minutes** serves **4**

2 medium peaches (300g), quartered,
  sliced thinly
2 medium nectarines (340g), quartered,
  sliced thinly
2 tablespoons light brown sugar
½ cup (80g) sultanas
1½ teaspoons ground cinnamon
½ teaspoon ground nutmeg
⅓ cup (25g) stale breadcrumbs
6 sheets fillo pastry
20g (¾ ounce) butter, melted
2 tablespoons milk
2 teaspoons icing (confectioners') sugar

1 Combine peach, nectarine, brown
sugar, sultanas, spices and breadcrumbs in
medium bowl.
2 Preheat oven to 200°C/400°F. Grease oven
tray; line with baking paper.
3 Stack fillo sheets, brushing all sheets with
half of the combined butter and milk. Cut fillo
stack in half widthways; cover one stack with
baking paper, then with a damp tea towel, to
prevent drying out.
4 Place half of the fruit mixture along centre of
uncovered fillo stack; roll from one side to
enclose filling, sealing ends of roll with a little of
the remaining butter mixture. Place strudel,
seam-side down, on tray; brush all over with a
little of the remaining butter mixture. Repeat
process with remaining fillo stack, fruit mixture
and butter mixture.
5 Bake strudels about 25 minutes or until
browned. Cut each strudel in half widthways;
divide among plates, dust with sifted icing sugar.

PORTUGUESE CUSTARD TARTS

prep + cook time **55 minutes** makes **12**

½ cup (110g) caster (superfine) sugar
2 tablespoons cornflour (cornstarch)
4 egg yolks
1¼ cups (310ml) pouring cream
⅓ cup (80ml) water
5cm (2-inch) strip lemon rind
1 teaspoon vanilla extract
1 sheet sweet puff pastry

1 Preheat oven to 220°C/425°F. Grease
12-hole (⅓-cup/80ml) muffin pan.
2 Combine sugar and cornflour in medium
saucepan; whisk in egg yolks, cream and the
water. Add rind; stir over medium heat until
mixture boils and thickens. Remove from heat;
discard rind. Stir extract into custard.
3 Cut pastry sheet in half; place halves on top
of each other. Roll pastry tightly from one short
side; cut roll into twelve 1cm (½-inch) rounds.
4 Place pastry rounds, cut-sides up, on floured
surface; roll each into a 10cm (4-inch) round.
Push rounds into pan holes; spoon in custard.
5 Bake tarts about 20 minutes. Stand 5
minutes, before lifting onto wire rack to cool.

tip **It's fine to use one 300ml carton of cream for this recipe.**

spiced stone fruit strudel

key lime pie

KEY LIME PIE

prep + cook time **45 minutes (+ refrigeration)** serves **8**

150g (4½ ounces) granita biscuits
80g (2½ ounces) butter, melted
4 egg yolks
395g (12½ ounces) canned sweetened
   condensed milk
1 tablespoon finely grated lime rind
½ cup (125ml) lime juice
1¼ cups (310ml) thickened (heavy) cream,
   whipped

1 Preheat oven to 180°C/350°F.
2 Process biscuits until fine, transfer to small
bowl; stir in butter. Press mixture over base and
side of 24cm (9½-inch) pie dish. Place dish on
oven tray; bake 10 minutes. Cool.
3 Beat egg yolks in small bowl with electric
mixer until light and fluffy. Beat in condensed
milk, rind and juice on low speed. Pour mixture
into crumb crust.
4 Bake pie about 12 minutes or until barely
set. Refrigerate 3 hours before serving. Serve
pie with cream or ice-cream.

tips **It's fine to use one 300ml carton of cream for this
recipe. This pie is traditionally made with key limes,
however they are a little hard to find in Australia so
we've used regular limes.**

PEAR TARTE TATIN

prep + cook time **1 hour 35 minutes (+ refrigeration)**
serves **6**

3 large firm pears (990g)
90g (3 ounces) butter, chopped
½ cup (110g) firmly packed light brown sugar
⅔ cup (160ml) pouring cream
¼ cup (35g) roasted pecans,
   chopped coarsely
pastry
1¼ cups (175g) plain (all-purpose) flour
⅓ cup (55g) icing (confectioners') sugar
90g (3 ounces) butter, chopped
1 egg yolk
1 tablespoon water

pear tarte tatin

1 Peel and core pears; cut lengthways
into quarters.
2 Melt butter with brown sugar in large frying
pan. Add cream, stirring, until sugar dissolves;
bring to the boil. Add pear, reduce heat;
simmer, turning occasionally, about 45 minutes
or until pear is tender.
3 Meanwhile, make pastry.
4 Preheat oven to 220°C/425°F.
5 Place pears, round-side down, in deep
22cm (9-inch) round cake pan; pour
caramelised pan liquid over pear, sprinkle
with nuts.
6 Roll pastry between sheets of baking paper
until slightly larger than circumference of
prepared pan. Remove top paper, turn pastry
onto pears. Remove remaining paper; tuck
pastry between pears and side of pan. Bake
about 25 minutes or until pastry is browned
lightly. Cool 5 minutes; turn tart onto serving
plate, serve with whipped cream.
pastry Blend or process flour, sugar and
butter until crumbly. Add egg yolk and the
water; process until ingredients come together.
Cover; refrigerate 30 minutes.

PECAN PIE

prep + cook time 1 hour 15 minutes (+ refrigeration)
serves 10

1 cup (120g) pecans, chopped coarsely
2 tablespoons cornflour (cornstarch)
1 cup (220g) firmly packed light brown sugar
60g (2 ounces) butter, melted
2 tablespoons pouring cream
1 teaspoon vanilla extract
3 eggs
⅓ cup (40g) pecans, extra
2 tablespoons apricot jam, warmed, sieved
pastry
1¼ cups (185g) plain (all-purpose) flour
⅓ cup (55g) icing (confectioners') sugar
125g (4 ounces) cold butter, chopped
1 egg yolk
1 teaspoon water

1 Make pastry.
2 Grease 24cm (9½-inch) round loose-based fluted flan tin. Roll pastry between sheets of baking paper until large enough to line tin. Lift pastry into tin; press into side, trim edge. Cover; refrigerate 20 minutes.
3 Preheat oven to 180°C/350°F.
4 Place tin on oven tray; line pastry with baking paper, fill with dried beans or rice. Bake 10 minutes. Remove paper and beans; bake about 5 minutes or until browned lightly. Cool.
5 Reduce oven to 160°C/325°F.
6 Combine chopped nuts and cornflour in medium bowl. Add sugar, butter, cream, extract and eggs; stir until combined. Pour mixture into pastry case, sprinkle with extra nuts.
7 Bake pie about 30 minutes. Cool; brush top of pie with jam.
pastry Process flour, icing sugar and butter until crumbly. Add egg yolk and the water; process until ingredients just come together. Knead dough on floured surface until smooth, enclose with plastic wrap; refrigerate 30 minutes.

APPLE PIE

prep + cook time **1 hour 45 minutes (+ refrigeration)**
serves **8**

10 medium apples (1.5kg)
½ cup (125ml) water
¼ cup (55g) caster (superfine) sugar
1 teaspoon finely grated lemon rind
¼ teaspoon ground cinnamon
1 egg white, beaten lightly
1 tablespoon caster (superfine) sugar, extra
pastry
1 cup (150g) plain (all-purpose) flour
½ cup (75g) self-raising flour
¼ cup (35g) cornflour (cornstarch)
¼ cup (30g) custard powder
1 tablespoon caster (superfine) sugar
100g (3 ounces) cold butter,
    chopped coarsely
1 egg yolk
¼ cup (60ml) iced water

1 Make pastry.
2 Peel, core and slice apple thickly. Place apple and the water in large saucepan; bring to the boil. Reduce heat; simmer, covered, 10 minutes or until apples soften. Drain; stir in sugar, rind and cinnamon. Cool.
3 Preheat oven to 220°C/425°F. Grease deep 24cm (9½-inch) pie dish.
4 Divide pastry in half. Roll one half between sheets of baking paper until large enough to line dish. Lift pastry into dish; press into base and side. Spoon apple mixture into pastry case; brush edge of pastry with egg white.
5 Roll remaining pastry large enough to cover filling; lift onto filling. Press edges together; trim away excess pastry. Brush pastry with egg white; sprinkle with extra sugar. Bake pie 20 minutes.
6 Reduce oven to 180°C/350°F; bake about 25 minutes or until golden brown. Serve with vanilla custard, or scoops of vanilla ice-cream.
pastry Process dry ingredients with the butter until crumbly. Add egg yolk and the water; process until ingredients come together. Knead dough on floured surface until smooth. Cover; refrigerate 30 minutes.

CHOCOLATE CUSTARD TARTS

prep + cook time **40 minutes** makes **24**

Preheat oven to 220°C/425°F. Grease two
12-hole (1-tablespoon/20ml) mini muffin pans.
Combine 3 egg yolks, ½ cup caster (superfine)
sugar, 2 tablespoons cornflour (cornstarch) and
1 tablespoon cocoa in medium saucepan;
whisk in ¾ cup milk and ⅔ cup pouring cream
until smooth. Stir over heat until mixture boils
and thickens; cool. Cut 1 sheet puff pastry in
half; stack two halves, press firmly. Roll pastry
up tightly from long side; cut log into 24 slices.
Roll slices between sheets of baking paper into
6cm (2½-inch) rounds; press rounds into pan
holes. Pour custard into pastry cases; bake
about 15 minutes. Cool in tin. Dust with sifted
icing (confectioners') sugar.

CARAMEL BANANA TART

prep + cook time **30 minutes** serves **16**

Preheat oven to 220°C/425°F. Place 1 sheet
puff pastry on greased oven tray. Fold edges
of pastry over to make a 1cm (½-inch) border
all the way around pastry. Prick pastry base
with fork. Place another oven tray on top of
pastry (this stops the pastry from puffing up
during baking); bake 10 minutes. Remove from
oven and take top tray off pastry. Meanwhile,
combine 20g (¾ ounce) butter, 2 tablespoons
light brown sugar and pinch ground cinnamon
in small saucepan; stir over low heat until
smooth. Combine butter mixture and 2 medium
thinly sliced bananas in medium bowl. Top tart
with banana mixture; bake about 10 minutes.
Cool 20 minutes before cutting.

EASY PUFF PIES

PEAR AND ALMOND GALETTES

prep + cook time **20 minutes** makes **4**

Preheat oven to 220°C/425°F. Grease
oven tray; line with baking paper. Combine
80g (2½ ounces) finely chopped dark eating
(semi-sweet) chocolate and 2 tablespoons
ground almonds in small bowl. Cut 1 sheet
puff pastry into quarters; place quarters on
oven tray, prick each with a fork, brush with
1 tablespoon milk. Divide chocolate mixture
over pastry squares, leaving 2cm (¾-inch)
border. Peel and core 1 medium pear; cut into
quarters. Cut each pear quarter into thin slices
then spread one sliced pear quarter across
each pastry square; sprinkle with 1 tablespoon
raw sugar then 1 tablespoon ground almonds.
Bake about 15 minutes.

ECCLES MINCE PIES

prep + cook time **45 minutes** makes **63**

Preheat oven to 200°C/400°F. Line oven trays
with baking paper. Cut 7 sheets puff pastry into
9 squares each. Divide 3½ cups fruit mince
between pastry squares; brush edges with
1 lightly beaten egg white. Gather pastry
edges together to enclose filling; place pies,
seam-side down on trays. Lightly flatten pies
with hand; cut two slits on top. Brush pies with
egg white; sprinkle with 1½ tablespoons white
(granulated) sugar. Bake about 15 minutes or
until browned lightly and puffed.

tip **Eccles pies are named after the English town of
Eccles and are traditionally filled with currants.**

MINI BERRY PIES

prep + cook time **45 minutes** makes **36**

Preheat oven to 200°C/400°F. Grease three 12-hole (1-tablespoon/20ml) mini muffin pans. Stir 300g (9½ ounces) frozen mixed berries and ¼ cup caster (superfine) sugar in small saucepan over low heat until sugar dissolves; bring to the boil. Blend 2 teaspoons cornflour (cornstarch) with 1 tablespoon water; stir into berry mixture. Stir over heat until mixture boils and thickens. Cool. Cut 36 x 6cm (2½-inch) rounds and 36 x 4cm (1½-inch) rounds from 5 sheets shortcrust pastry; press large pastry rounds into pan holes. Spoon berry mixture into pastry cases; top with small pastry rounds. Press edges firmly to seal. Brush tops with 1 lightly beaten egg white; sprinkle with 1 tablespoon caster (superfine) sugar. Make small cut in top of each pie. Bake pies about 20 minutes. Stand in pan 10 minutes before turning, top-side up, onto wire rack.

CHOC-NUT APPLE TURNOVERS

prep + cook time **30 minutes** makes **16**

Preheat oven to 190°C/375°F. Grease oven trays; line with baking paper. Cut 2 small peeled apples into eight wedges each; remove cores. Cut 16 x 10cm (4-inch) rounds from 4 sheets shortcrust pastry. Divide ⅓ cup chocolate hazelnut spread into centre of pastry rounds; top each with an apple wedge. Brush edges with a little beaten egg white; fold rounds in half to enclose filling, pinch edges to seal. Place on trays. Brush turnovers with egg white; sprinkle with 1 tablespoon white (granulated) sugar. Bake about 20 minutes. Transfer to wire rack to cool.

EASY SHORTCRUST PIES

LEMON MERINGUE TARTLETS

prep + cook time **15 minutes** makes **12**

Preheat oven to 180°C/350°F. Place 12 (275g) small frozen sweet shortcrust tart cases on oven tray; bake cases 10 minutes, cool. Increase oven to 240°C/425°F. Spoon 340g (11 ounces) lemon curd into tart cases. Beat 3 egg whites in small bowl with electric mixer until soft peaks form; gradually add ¾ cup caster (superfine) sugar, beating until sugar dissolves. Pipe or spoon meringue over lemon curd. Bake tarts about 5 minutes or until meringue is browned lightly.

BUTTERSCOTCH TARTLETS

prep + cook time **15 minutes (+ refrigeration)** makes **12**

Place 12 (275g) small frozen sweet shortcrust tart cases on oven tray; bake cases 10 minutes, cool. Meanwhile, stir ¼ cup firmly packed light brown sugar, 20g (¾ ounce) butter and ¼ cup pouring cream in small saucepan until sugar dissolves. Simmer, uncovered, without stirring, 2 minutes. Cool 5 minutes. Stir in 150g (4½ ounces) coarsely chopped dark eating (semi-sweet) chocolate and another ¼ cup pouring cream; refrigerate 10 minutes. Spoon mixture into tartlet cases; sprinkle with 2 tablespoons coarsely chopped roasted hazelnuts and 1 tablespoon sifted cocoa powder.

BERRY COULIS

prep + cook time **10 minutes** serves **4**

Push 300g (9½ ounces) thawed frozen
strawberries through fine sieve into small bowl;
discard seeds. Stir in 1 tablespoon sifted icing
(confectioners') sugar.

tips **Any berries, fresh or frozen, can be used; blend or
process berries until smooth, then continue as above.
Other fruits such as mango, passionfruit, kiwifruit, and
even guava or pineapple, can be used. Sugar needs to
be adjusted according to the fruit used.**

RHUBARB AND PEAR COMPOTE

prep + cook time **15 minutes** serves **4**

Combine 2 cups coarsely chopped rhubarb,
1 coarsely chopped medium pear, ¼ cup
caster (superfine) sugar, 2 tablespoons water
and 1 teaspoon mixed spice in medium
saucepan; bring to the boil. Reduce heat;
simmer, stirring occasionally, about 5 minutes
or until fruit softens slightly.

BANANA AND HAZELNUT TOPPING

prep + cook time **10 minutes** serves **4**

Stir 100g (3 ounces) coarsely chopped milk
eating chocolate, 10g (½ ounce) butter and
½ cup pouring cream in small saucepan over
low heat until smooth. Drizzle chocolate sauce
over ice-cream of your choice; top with 2 thinly
sliced medium bananas and ¼ cup coarsely
chopped roasted hazelnuts.

FUDGE SAUCE

prep + cook time **15 minutes** serves **4**

Stir 200g (6½ ounces) coarsely chopped dark
eating (semi-sweet) chocolate and 20g
(¾ ounce) butter in small heatproof bowl set
over small saucepan of simmering water (do
not allow water to touch base of bowl) until
smooth. Add ¼ teaspoon vanilla extract and
½ cup pouring cream; stir until combined.
Serve sauce warm.

tip **Sauce will keep under refrigeration, covered, for up
to three days. To serve, reheat sauce briefly in
microwave oven on HIGH (100%) or over low heat in
small saucepan until it reaches the desired consistency.**

ICE-CREAM TOPPINGS

COFFEE LIQUEUR SAUCE

prep + cook time **20 minutes (+ refrigeration)** serves **6**

Combine ¼ cup pouring cream and ⅔ cup freshly brewed strong coffee in small saucepan; stir over medium heat, without boiling, until hot. Remove from heat; add 250g (8 ounces) coarsely chopped white eating chocolate, whisk until smooth. Stir in 1 tablespoon coffee-flavoured liqueur. Transfer sauce to small bowl; cover, refrigerate about 30 minutes, stirring occasionally.

ORANGE BUTTERSCOTCH SAUCE

prep + cook time **15 minutes** serves **4**

Stir ½ cup thickened (heavy) cream, ½ cup firmly packed light brown sugar, 60g (2 ounces) butter and 1 teaspoon finely grated orange rind in small saucepan over heat, without boiling, until sugar dissolves; bring to the boil. Reduce heat; simmer, uncovered, 3 minutes.

tip **Orange butterscotch sauce will keep for up to two days in an airtight container in the refrigerator.**

CARAMEL SAUCE

prep + cook time **25 minutes** serves **6**

Stir 1 cup caster (superfine) sugar and ½ cup water in small saucepan over low heat until sugar dissolves; bring to the boil.
Boil, uncovered, without stirring, about 15 minutes or until mixture turns a caramel colour. Remove from heat; allow bubbles to subside. Gradually add 1¼ cups pouring cream, stirring constantly, over low heat, until sauce is smooth. Cool 10 minutes.

tip **It's fine to use one 300ml carton of cream for this recipe.**

COCONUT AND ORANGE SAUCE

prep + cook time **15 minutes** serves **4**

Place ⅔ cup pouring cream, 10cm (4-inch) strip orange rind and 2 bruised cardamom pods in small saucepan; bring to the boil. Remove from heat. Add 180g (5½ ounces) coarsely chopped white eating chocolate and 2 teaspoons coconut-flavoured liqueur; stir until smooth. Strain sauce; discard cinnamon and rind.

tips **We used Malibu but you can use any coconut-flavoured liqueur you like. A citrus-flavoured liqueur, such as Grand Marnier, can be substituted for the Malibu.**

ALLSPICE also known as pimento or jamaican pepper; is so named because it tastes like a combination of nutmeg, cumin, cinnamon and clove. It is available whole or ground, from most supermarkets and specialty spice stores.

ALMONDS

blanched almonds with brown skins removed.

flaked paper-thin slices.

ground also known as almond meal.

slivered small pieces cut lengthways.

BAKING POWDER a raising agent consisting mainly of two parts cream of tartar to one part bicarbonate of soda (baking soda).

BICARBONATE OF SODA also known as baking soda; a mild alkali used as a leavening agent in baking.

BREADCRUMBS

fresh bread, usually white, processed into crumbs.

packaged prepared fine-textured but crunchy white breadcrumbs; good for coating foods that are to be fried.

stale crumbs made by grating, blending or processing 1- or 2-day-old bread.

BUTTER we use salted butter unless stated; 125g is equal to 1 stick (4 ounces). Unsalted or "sweet" butter has no salt added and is perhaps the most popular among pastry chefs.

BUTTERMILK originally the term for the slightly sour liquid left after butter was churned from cream, today it is made like yogurt. Sold with milk products in supermarkets. Despite the implication, it is low in fat.

CARDAMOM a spice native to India and used extensively in its cuisine; can be purchased in pod, seed or ground form. Has a distinctive aromatic, sweetly rich flavour and is one of the world's most expensive spices. Used to flavour curries, rice dishes, sweet desserts and cakes.

CASHEWS plump, kidney-shaped, golden-brown nuts with a distinctive sweet, buttery flavour and containing about 48 per cent fat. Due to their high fat content they should be stored in the refrigerator to avoid becoming rancid.

CHOC BITS also known as chocolate chips or chocolate morsels; available in milk, white and dark chocolate. Made of cocoa liquor, cocoa butter, sugar and an emulsifier, these hold their shape in baking and are ideal for decorating.

CHOCOLATE

dark eating also called semi-sweet or luxury chocolate; made of a high percentage of cocoa liquor and cocoa butter, and little added sugar. Unless stated otherwise, we use dark eating chocolate in this book as it's ideal for use in desserts and cakes.

melts small discs of compounded milk, white or dark chocolate ideal for melting and moulding.

milk most popular eating chocolate, mild and very sweet; similar in make-up to dark with the difference being the addition of milk solids.

white eating contains no cocoa solids but derives its sweet flavour from cocoa butter. Very sensitive to heat.

CHOCOLATE HAZELNUT SPREAD also known as Nutella; made of cocoa powder, hazelnuts, sugar and milk.

CINNAMON available in pieces (called sticks or quills) and ground into powder; one of the world's most common spices, it is used as a sweet, fragrant flavouring for sweet and savoury dishes.

COCOA POWDER also known as unsweetened cocoa; cocoa beans (cacao seeds) that have been fermented, roasted, shelled, ground into powder then cleared of most of the fat content.

COCONUT

cream obtained commercially from the first pressing of the coconut flesh alone, without the addition of water; the second pressing (less rich) is sold as coconut milk. Available in cans and cartons at most supermarkets.

desiccated concentrated, dried, unsweetened and finely shredded coconut flesh.

flaked dried flaked coconut flesh.

milk not the liquid found inside the fruit (coconut water) but the diluted liquid from the second pressing of the white flesh of a mature coconut. Available in cans and cartons at most supermarkets.

shredded unsweetened thin strips of dried coconut flesh.

COOKING SPRAY we use a cholesterol-free spray made from canola oil.

CORNFLOUR also known as cornstarch. Available made from corn or wheat (wheaten cornflour, gluten-free, gives a lighter texture in cakes).

CREAM we use fresh pouring cream, also known as pure cream. It has no additives, and contains a minimum fat content of 35 per cent.

GLOSSARY

pouring also called pure cream. It has no additives, and contains a minimum fat content of 35 per cent.

thickened a whipping cream that contains a thickener (minimum fat content of 35 per cent).

sour thick, commercially-cultured sour cream with a minimum fat content of 35 per cent.

CREME FRAICHE a mature, naturally fermented cream (minimum 35 per cent fat content) with a velvety texture and slightly tangy, nutty flavour. It can boil without curdling.

CUSTARD POWDER instant mixture used to make pouring custard; similar to North American instant pudding mixes.

DATES fruit of the date palm tree, eaten fresh or dried, on their own or in prepared dishes. About 4cm to 6cm in length, oval and plump, thin-skinned, with a honey-sweet flavour and sticky texture. Best known, perhaps, for their inclusion in sticky toffee pudding; also found in muesli; muffins, scones and cakes; compotes and stewed fruit desserts.

EGGS we use large chicken eggs weighing an average of 60g unless stated otherwise. If a recipe calls for raw or barely cooked eggs, take care if there is a salmonella problem in your area, particularly in food eaten by children and pregnant women.

FIGS originally from the countries that border the eastern Mediterranean; best eaten in peak season, at the height of summer. Vary in skin and flesh colour according to type not ripeness: the purple-black mission or black mission fig, with pink flesh, is a rich-flavoured, good all-rounder.

FLOUR

plain also known as all-purpose; unbleached wheat flour is the best for baking: the gluten content ensures a strong dough, which produces a light result.

rice very fine, almost powdery, gluten-free flour; made from ground white rice. Used in baking, as a thickener, and in some Asian noodles and desserts.

self-raising also known as self-rising flour. Make at home in the proportion of 1 cup plain (all-purpose) flour to 2 teaspoons baking powder.

GELATINE we use dried (powdered) gelatine in the recipes in this book; it's also available in sheet form known as leaf gelatine. A thickening agent made from either collagen, a protein found in animal connective tissue and bones, or certain algae (agar-agar). Three teaspoons of dried gelatine (8g or one sachet) is roughly equivalent to four gelatine leaves. Professionals use leaf gelatine because it generally results in a smoother, clearer consistency; it is also most commonly used throughout Europe. The two types are interchangable but leaf gelatine gives a much clearer mixture than dried gelatine; it's perfect in dishes where appearance really counts.

GINGER

ground also called powdered ginger; cannot be substituted for fresh.

GLACE FRUIT fruit such as pineapple, apricots, peaches and pears that are cooked in a heavy sugar syrup then dried.

GOLDEN SYRUP a by-product of refined sugarcane; pure maple syrup or honey can be substituted.

HAZELNUTS also known as filberts; plump, grape-sized, rich, sweet nut with a brown skin that is removed by rubbing heated nuts together vigorously in a tea-towel.

ground also called meal; hazelnuts ground to a coarse flour texture.

LIQUEUR

citrus-flavoured liqueur such as grand marnier and cointreau.

coconut-flavoured such as Malibu.

coffee-flavoured such as Tia Maria or Kahlua.

MACADAMIAS native to Australia; fairly large, slightly soft, buttery rich nut. Refrigerate nuts to prevent them turning rancid (due to their high oil content).

MAPLE SYRUP distilled from the sap of sugar maple trees, which are found only in Canada and about ten states in the USA. Most often eaten with pancakes or waffles, but also used as an ingredient in baking or in preparing desserts. Maple-flavoured syrup or pancake syrup is not an adequate substitute for the real thing.

MAPLE-FLAVOURED SYRUP is made from sugar cane and is also known as golden or pancake syrup. It is not a substitute for pure maple syrup.

MARMALADE a preserve, usually based on citrus fruit and its rind, cooked with sugar until the mixture has an intense flavour and thick consistency. Orange, lemon and lime are some of the commercially prepared varieties available.

MILK we use full-cream homogenised milk unless otherwise specified.

sweetened condensed a canned milk product consisting of milk with more than half the water content removed and sugar added to the remaining milk.

MIXED DRIED FRUIT a combination of sultanas, raisins, currants, mixed peel and cherries.

MIXED SPICE a classic mixture generally containing caraway, allspice, coriander, cumin, nutmeg and ginger, although cinnamon and other spices can be added. It is used with fruit and in cakes.

NUTMEG a strong and pungent spice ground from the dried nut of an evergreen tree native to Indonesia. Usually found ground but the flavour is more intense from a whole nut, available from spice shops, so it's best to grate your own. Used most often in baking and milk-based desserts, but also works nicely in savoury dishes. Found in mixed spice mixtures.

PAPRIKA ground dried sweet red capsicum (bell pepper); there are many grades and varieties, including hot, mild, sweet and smoked.

PEANUTS also known as groundnut, not in fact a nut but the pod of a legume. We mainly use raw (unroasted) or unsalted roasted peanuts.

PECANS native to the US and now grown locally; pecans are golden brown, buttery and rich. Good in savoury as well as sweet dishes; walnuts are a good substitute.

PISTACHIOS green, delicately flavoured nuts inside hard off-white shells. Available salted or unsalted in or out of shells.

QUINCE yellow-skinned fruit with hard texture and astringent, tart taste; eaten cooked or as a preserve. Long, slow cooking makes the flesh a deep rose pink.

RAISINS dried sweet grapes (traditionally muscatel grapes).

RHUBARB classified as a vegetable, is eaten as a fruit and therefore considered one. Leaves must be removed before cooking as they can contain traces of poison; the edible crisp, pink-red stalks are cooked.

ROLLED OATS flattened oat grain rolled into flakes and traditionally used for porridge. Instant oats are also available, but traditional oats are best for baking.

ROSEWATER extract made from crushed rose petals, called gulab in India; used for its aromatic quality in many sweetmeats and desserts.

RUM we use a dark underproof rum (not overproof) for a more subtle flavour in cooking. White rum is almost colourless, sweet and used mostly in drinks.

SPONGE FINGER BISCUITS also known as savoiardi, savoy biscuits or lady's fingers, they are Italian-style crisp fingers made from sponge cake mixture.

STAR ANISE a dried star-shaped pod whose seeds have an astringent aniseed flavour; commonly used to flavour stocks and marinades.

SUGAR

brown a very soft, fine granulated sugar retaining molasses for colour and flavour.

caster also called superfine or finely granulated table sugar; dissolves easily.

icing also known as confectioners' sugar or powdered sugar; pulverised granulated sugar crushed together with a small amount of cornflour.

palm also called nam tan pip, jaggery, jawa or gula melaka; made from the sap of the sugar palm tree. Light brown to black in colour and usually sold in rock-hard cakes; use brown sugar if unavailable.

pure icing also known as confectioners' sugar or powdered sugar.

raw natural brown granulated sugar.

VANILLA

bean dried, long, thin pod from a tropical golden orchid grown in central and South America and Tahiti; the minuscule black seeds inside the bean are used to impart a luscious vanilla flavour in baking and desserts. Place a whole bean in a jar of sugar to make the vanilla sugar often called for in recipes; a bean can be used three or four times.

extract obtained from vanilla beans infused in water; a non-alcoholic version of essence. It is found in most supermarkets in the baking section.

WALNUTS fruit of the walnut tree, walnuts can be bought all year round, in or out of their shells. They will keep longer in their shells. Walnuts are rich in omega-3 fatty acids and are a good source of fibre. They are great in salads and cakes and are a healthy additive to breakfast cereal or porridge.

YEAST (dried and fresh), a raising agent used in dough making. Granular (7g sachets) and fresh compressed (20g blocks) yeast can almost always be substituted one for the other when yeast is called for.

YOGURT we use plain full-cream yogurt unless stated otherwise.

CONVERSION CHART

MEASURES

One Australian metric measuring cup holds approximately 250ml, one Australian metric tablespoon holds 20ml, one Australian metric teaspoon holds 5ml.

The difference between one country's measuring cups and another's is within a 2- or 3-teaspoon variance, and will not affect your cooking results. North America, New Zealand and the United Kingdom use a 15ml tablespoon. All cup and spoon measurements are level. The most accurate way of measuring dry ingredients is to weigh them. When measuring liquids, use a clear glass or plastic jug with metric markings.

We use large eggs with an average weight of 60g.

DRY MEASURES

METRIC	IMPERIAL
15g	½oz
30g	1oz
60g	2oz
90g	3oz
125g	4oz (¼lb)
155g	5oz
185g	6oz
220g	7oz
250g	8oz (½lb)
280g	9oz
315g	10oz
345g	11oz
375g	12oz (¾lb)
410g	13oz
440g	14oz
470g	15oz
500g	16oz (1lb)
750g	24oz (1½lb)
1kg	32oz (2lb)

LIQUID MEASURES

METRIC	IMPERIAL
30ml	1 fluid oz
60ml	2 fluid oz
100ml	3 fluid oz
125ml	4 fluid oz
150ml	5 fluid oz
190ml	6 fluid oz
250ml	8 fluid oz
300ml	10 fluid oz
500ml	16 fluid oz
600ml	20 fluid oz
1000ml (1 litre)	1¾ pints

LENGTH MEASURES

METRIC	IMPERIAL
3mm	⅛in
6mm	¼in
1cm	½in
2cm	¾in
2.5cm	1in
5cm	2in
6cm	2½in
8cm	3in
10cm	4in
13cm	5in
15cm	6in
18cm	7in
20cm	8in
23cm	9in
25cm	10in
28cm	11in
30cm	12in (1ft)

OVEN TEMPERATURES

These oven temperatures are only a guide for conventional ovens.
For fan-forced ovens, check the manufacturer's manual.

	°C (CELSIUS)	°F (FAHRENHEIT)
Very slow	120	250
Slow	150	275-300
Moderately slow	160	325
Moderate	180	350-375
Moderately hot	200	400
Hot	220	425-450
Very hot	240	475

The imperial measurements used in these recipes are approximate only. Measurements for cake pans are approximate only. Using same-shaped cake pans of a similar size should not affect the outcome of your baking. We measure the inside top of the cake pan to determine sizes.

INDEX

First Published in 2011 by ACP Magazines Ltd,
a division of Nine Entertainment Co.

54 Park St, Sydney

GPO Box 4088, Sydney, NSW 2001.

phone (02) 9282 8618; fax (02) 9267 9438

acpbooks@acpmagazines.com.au; www.acpbooks.com.au

ACP BOOKS

General Manager - Christine Whiston

Associate Publisher - Seymour Cohen

Editor-in-Chief - Susan Tomnay

Creative Director - Hieu Chi Nguyen

Food Director - Pamela Clark

Published and Distributed in the United Kingdom by Octopus Publishing Group

Endeavour House

189 Shaftesbury Avenue

London WC2H 8JY

United Kingdom

phone (+44)(0)207 632 5400; fax (+44)(0)207 632 5405

info@octopus-publishing.co.uk;

www.octopusbooks.co.uk

Printed by Toppan Printing Co., China

International foreign language rights, Brian Cearnes, ACP Books bcearnes@acpmagazines.com.au

A catalogue record for this book is available from the British Library.

ISBN 978-1-74245-137-4